PAPER ENGINEERING

NTRODUCTION

Every time you pick up a piece of card packaging or a pop-up book or greeting card, you're holding an example of paper engineering.

This book has been written to help you develop design ideas using paper engineering techniques. It contains two main sections.

In the first section you will be introduced to some of the elements of paper engineering. You will come across
■ examples of techniques and methods of construction
■ suggestions to explore that will help you make use of the techniques you have learned.

In the second section you will find a number of challenges. Each of these offers you a range of starting points for designing activities using paper and card.

On this page and the following one you will find information about the basic skills you will need to use when working with this book. Look at them now, and make sure you understand the things you will be asked to do.

You may also have access to some templates which go with the book; these are printed sheets which let you quickly and easily make up examples of the structures and mechanisms in the book. These templates are separate from the book, so ask your teacher about them.

Cutting

To cut paper or card, you can use scissors or a craft knife. Scissors are more useful for cutting outside curves and slits which are open at one end. Knives are more useful for cutting straight edges, when used with a ruler—preferably a safety ruler. They are also best for cutting out any shape or slot in the middle of pieces of paper or card—using scissors for this will distort your work.

You may have access to a disc cutter, in which the wheel rotates as it cuts. This is very useful for cutting curves, but be **very** careful—the disc is usually super-sharp!

To cut circles in card, you can use a circle cutter which works like a pair of compasses. Small circles can be cut neatly with wad punches which are available in a range of diameters. Very small

holes can be made with punch pliers, as well as with the smaller sizes of wad punches.

Whatever you're cutting, remember; your skin cuts much more easily than card or paper! **Take care**. And always make sure you use a cutting mat or pad underneath your work.

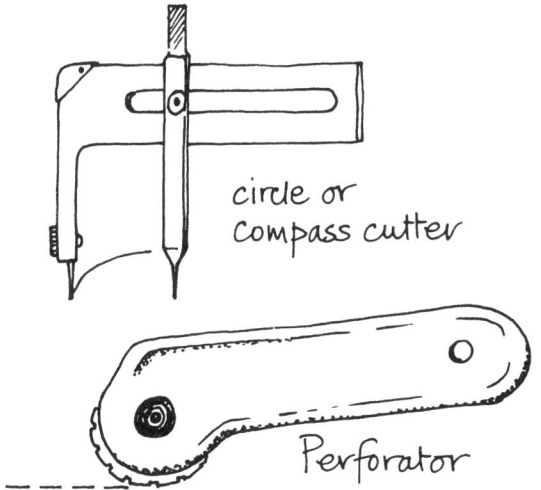

circle or compass cutter

Perforator

Scoring, perforating and folding

Card folds much more easily and accurately if you either score or perforate it first. Many of the construction methods you will come across depend on accurate folding to work properly. Applying the techniques shown here with care and patience will save you much frustration when you come to assemble your work.

Straight lines can be scored along a ruler, but a more effective method is to use a scoring guide. You can make scoring guides to fit any outline using the method shown—this is something you should try. Remember, it's usually easier to fold away from the scored line, so try to score on the outside of the fold.

An alternative way of making sure your paper or card folds where you want it to is to use a perforating tool. This consists of a wheel with regular nicks in the cutting edge, mounted on the end of a handle; as you wheel it across paper or card it leaves a line of perforations along which you can fold. The perforator is really a cutting tool, so make sure you use it on a cutting mat or pad.

If your scoring or perforating is careful and accurate, folding is unlikely to be a problem.

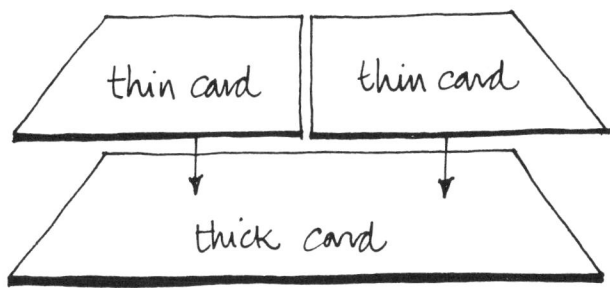

To make a scoring guide glue two pieces of thin card to a piece of thicker card or greyboard so that there is a narrow gap between them.

To crease or score your card place it over the gap in the scoring guide and press the edge of a ruler along the crease.

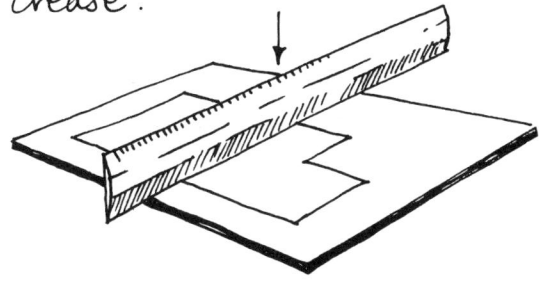

Glueing

It's very important to choose the right glue, because some of the glues which are available to you will distort your work. These mainly include the water-based glues like PVA. Spirit-based glues like UHU or Bostik All-purpose give cleaner and smoother results.

Other alternatives include glue sticks such as Pritt or Pelifix, and double-sided sticky tape. These are both relatively clean and straightforward to use.

The spirit-based glues and glue sticks allow a short period for readjustment before sticking fast. Double-sided sticky tape holds immediately and permanently—there's no second chance!

The best and simplest way of holding paper or card together while glueing is by hand. Sometimes it's helpful to have some gripping tools available; these could include paper clips, bulldog clips, clothes pegs, or any other similar device. Occasionally masking tape or blu-tack is useful.

Accuracy is most important when glueing your mechanisms or structures together. If you get glue in the wrong place it will prevent you from assembling your work accurately, and it will stop it from working properly. At the very least badly glued work looks messy, and the glue can spoil the quality of the surface finish.

If you are adding lettering or colour to your design, you will find this much easier to do before final assembly and glueing.

3

 OILS

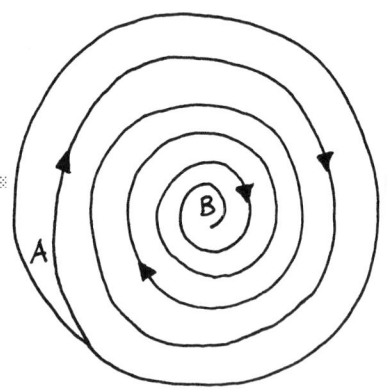

Coils are possibly the simplest way of creating a moving action in a pop-up card or book. Although they are usually used in combination with other mechanisms or structures, they can also be very effective on their own.

The coil creates a lot of movement from a very simple shape. To create the effect simply cut out a shape—a circle will do, but many different shapes work well, so experiment.

Starting at any point on the edge of the shape, draw a continuous line which spirals towards the centre. Next, cut carefully along this line. You should now have a card coil which can be pulled out like a spring.

This can be used in a card or book by simply glueing one end of the coil to the left-hand page, and the other end to the right-hand page so that when the card or book is closed, the coil lies flat. When you open the pages, the coil is opened and is allowed to spring out. Different effects can be achieved by using different thicknesses of card.

If you are careful, other images and shapes can be fixed at points along this coil. As the pages open, they will dance and move.

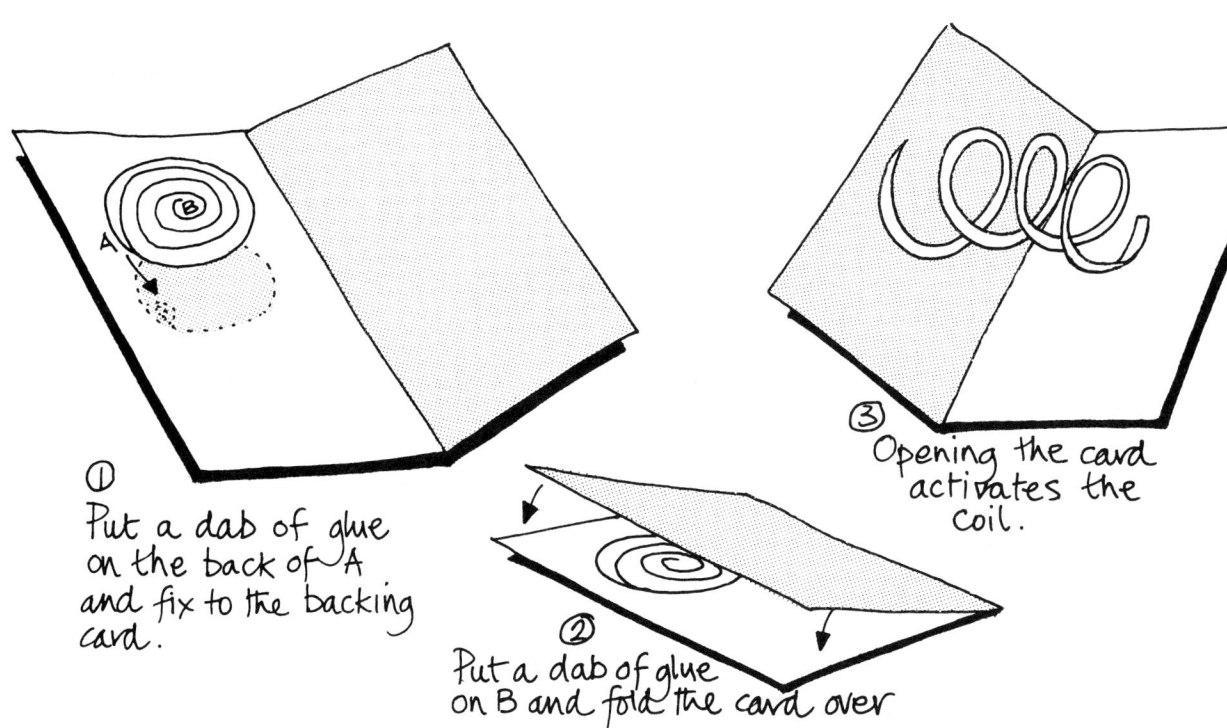

① Put a dab of glue on the back of A and fix to the backing card.

② Put a dab of glue on B and fold the card over

③ Opening the card activates the coil.

EXPLORATIONS

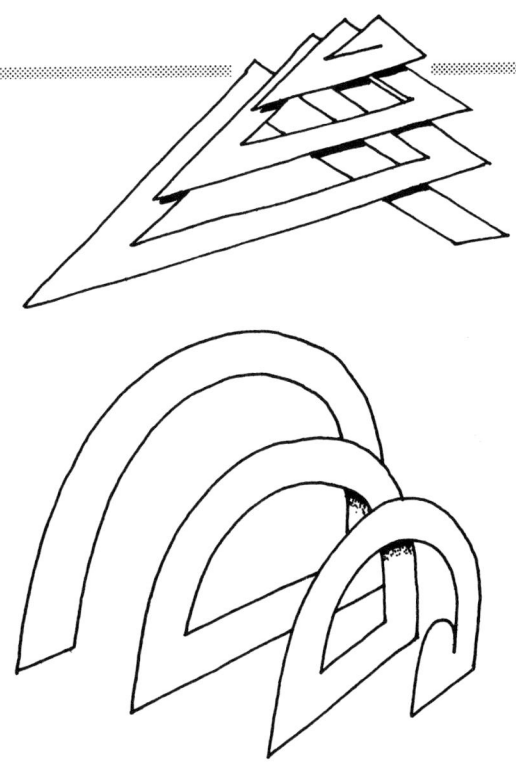

You can make a spiral coil from many different shapes; try some of these—a triangle, a square, a hexagon, or any irregular shape with a number of straight edges. Curved shapes can also be used—try an ellipse or a semi-circle.

Natural shapes, drawn freehand, can be just as good. Try a cloud, a simple leaf, a fruit—any natural shape should work.

Your coil does not need to taper from the outside to the centre. You can make a helix, which is a coil with a parallel profile (see the diagram), by cutting a number of identical card rings and glueing them end to end. This kind of coil does not lie completely flat when assembled. Of course the card rings don't have to be circular—you can experiment with shapes. Use your original ring as an outline to cut around to make sure all other rings are identical.

Try experimenting further with shape. Design a coil which changes from one shape to another by stages—from a circle to a triangle, say—throughout its length. Here each ring would be different, and would change shape gradually in sequence.

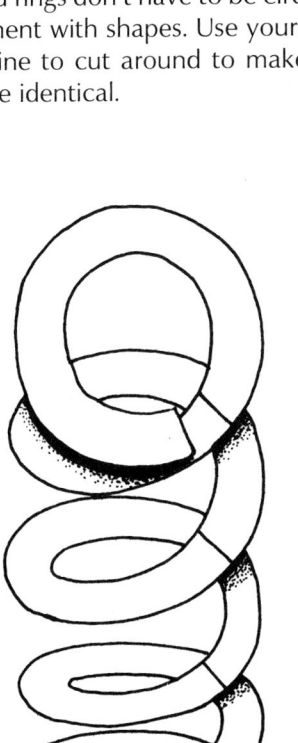

Can this 'helix' type coil be made from any other shapes?

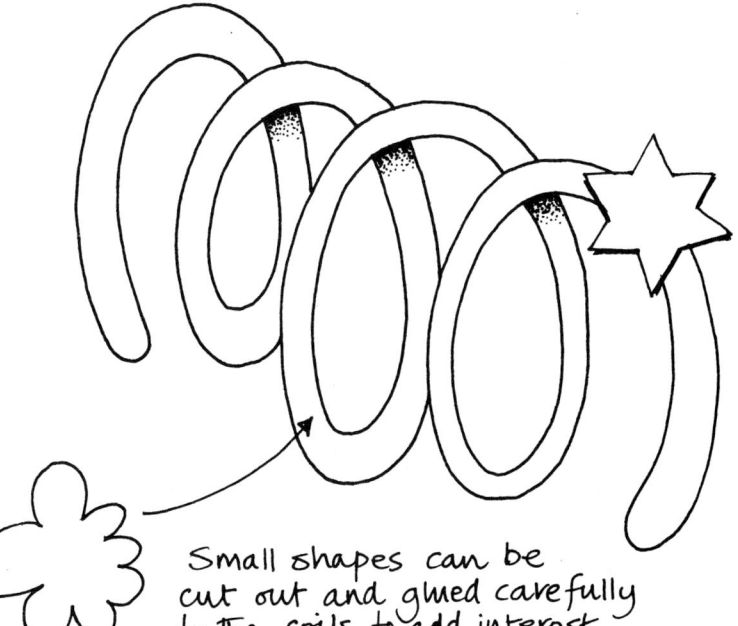

Small shapes can be cut out and glued carefully to the coils to add interest.

5

PARALLEL SURFACES

Parallel Surfaces

Pop-up books and cards make great use of these techniques, which let you create vertical or horizontal surfaces raised from a background either one or several at a time. Although the techniques are similar, the end results are very different.

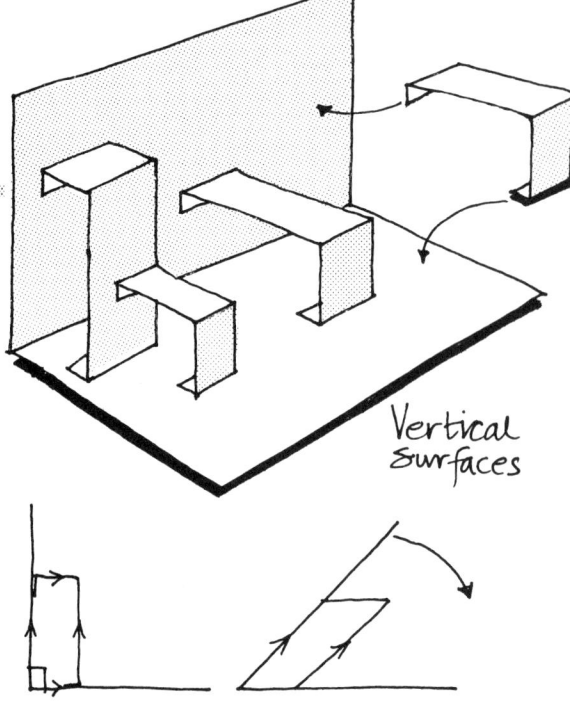

Vertical Surfaces

Method 1

Method 1 is used with books or cards which open to 90° (as opposed to 180°, which is opened out flat). Each surface is connected to the card or page by spacing tabs which keeps it parallel to one of the base surfaces when the book or card is opened.

Several raised surfaces can be used together, but the more you use, and the greater the thickness of card, the harder it is to close the whole thing flat. A number of surfaces at different distances from the base can give the feeling of depth and distance.

Often vertical surfaces are used to support other images or shapes which stand up when the book or card is opened.

Make sure that the surface does not stick out when the card is closed. How can you work out the correct size?

Horizontal Surfaces

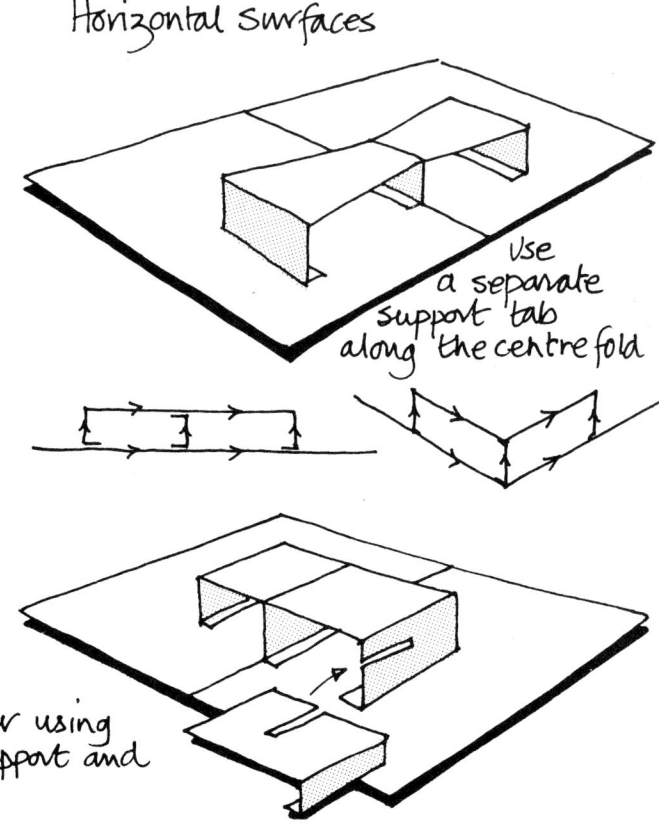

Use a separate support tab along the centre fold

Method 2

This too creates surfaces which remain parallel to a base. Here the whole base surface is flat when open, like a book opened flat (though you can of course stand it up vertically if you want. It could for example hang from a wall). The supported surface crosses the fold and at least three spacing tabs are needed, which must all be the same length. Two of the spacing tabs must be positioned on one side of the fold, and one or more on the other (see diagrams).

Several surfaces can be built up in layers, supporting each other, using this technique. Slotted hinges and supports make it possible for one spacing tab to do the work of several.

Second layer using a slot for support and hinge.

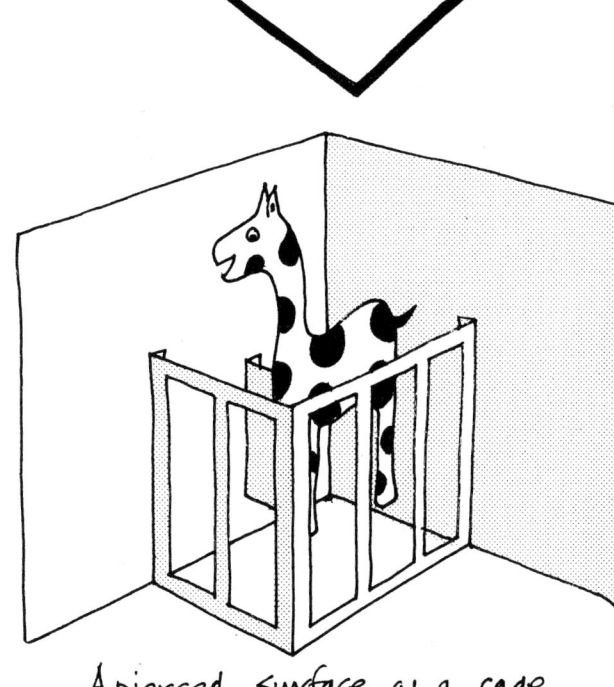

EXPLORATIONS

Method 1

If you have a template for these structures make it up now. Otherwise make up an example of the two structures from the information opposite. You are now in a position to

■ experiment with sizes. How far can a surface stand out from the base before it becomes visible when the assembly is closed up? How near the edge of the base can you take the fixing point for the spacing tabs?

■ try some variations. What happens when you pierce surfaces with holes (windows)? Can you think of ways to make use of this effect—to increase the sense of depth, perhaps, or to create visual interest?

Method 2

Again, you should make up an example, and then

■ **either** develop your own design for an outline shape which suggests something that flies or hovers (dragonfly, seagull, harrier jet), seen from above. Make a card model in which this shape hovers above the base plane.

■ **or** mount it vertically and create a view into a room through a window.

A pierced surface as a cage.

Other shapes can be glued onto the surfaces

 -FOLD

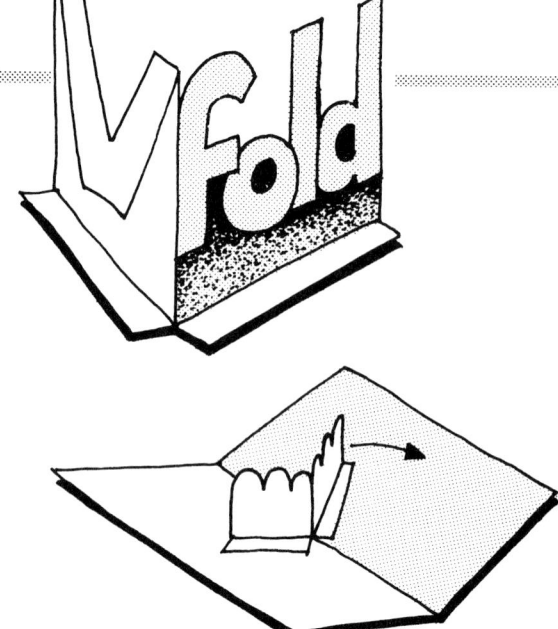

The V-fold mechanism is a most useful method of creating a pop-up movement. It is used to good effect in many pop-up books and cards.

The mechanism gets its name from the V-shape that it forms. It must be arranged so that it is symmetrical along the centre-fold of the card or book. Look at the illustrations to get an idea of what symmetrical means here. The mechanism works by opening and closing the card.

The V can be made to fold either forwards or backwards depending on the position of the spacing tabs. The spacing tabs can be hidden or made into a feature of the design.

You can make V-folds stand up straight when the book or card is open, or you can make them lean forward or backward. This is done by changing the angle between the central fold and the fixing flap folds. If this angle is 90° the V-fold will stand up straight; if it is more or less than 90° it will lean (see the diagrams).

There are many ways of using the V-fold, some of which are shown here.

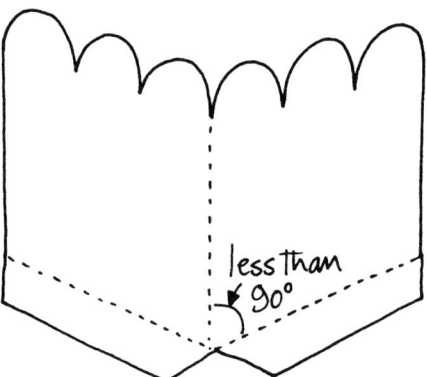

This 'V' fold will move forwards when closed. Can you make it move backwards?

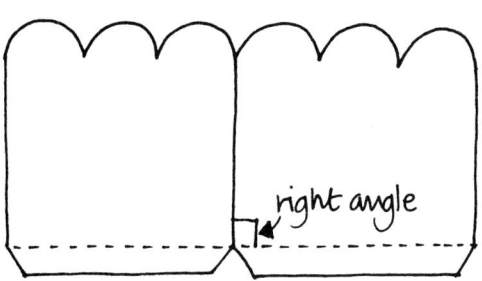

This way makes the 'V' fold stand straight up.

Does this make the 'V' fold slope backwards or forwards? Experiment with different angles.

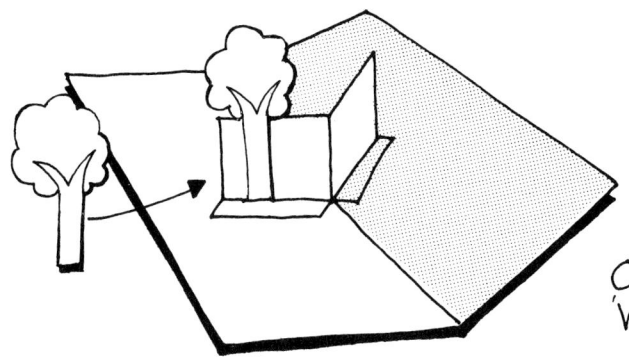

Other shapes can be cut out in the 'V' or glued to it.

EXPLORATIONS

Once you have made up a basic example (either by copying or from a template), try some of the following variations:

■ two or more V-folds on the same card, mounting

■ some of them pointing up rather than down. What happens when you cut part of the V-fold away? Which bits cannot be removed?

Can you combine the V-fold with either of the techniques you have already come across (coils or horizontal or vertical surfaces)? Can you make a parallel surface work from a V-fold? Are there any snags in doing this?

arch or bridge →

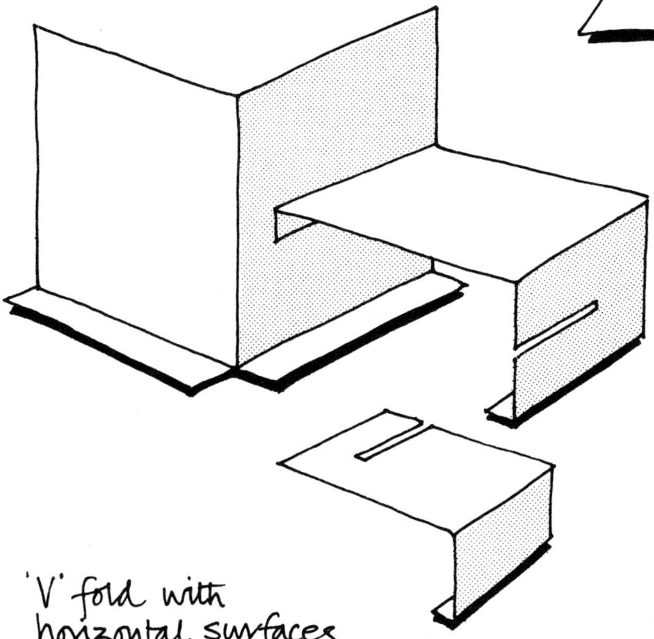

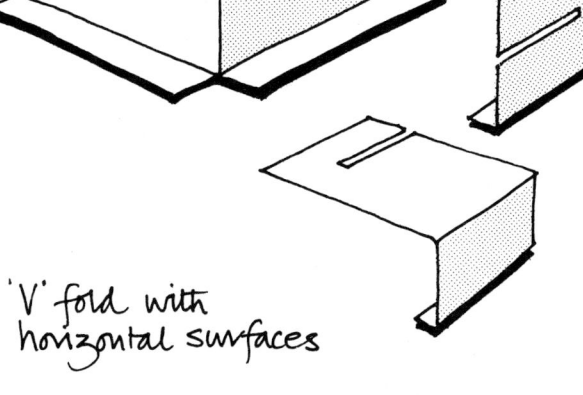

'V' fold with horizontal surfaces

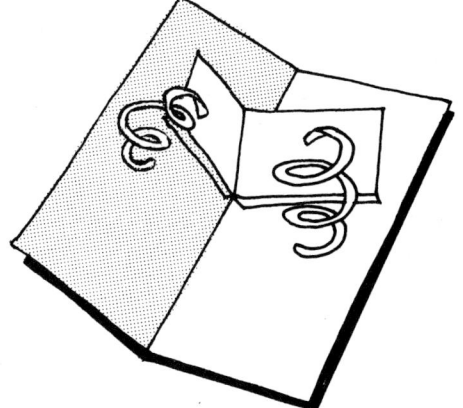

'V' fold with coils

V-FOLD AND FLYING ARM

A slightly different kind of V-fold can be used as the basis for mounting another image or to create a flying arm effect. This effect creates a large amount of movement and can be made in three different ways.

Method 1

This method involves cutting and folding a V-fold in the backing card itself and then attaching the flying arm to one side of the V.

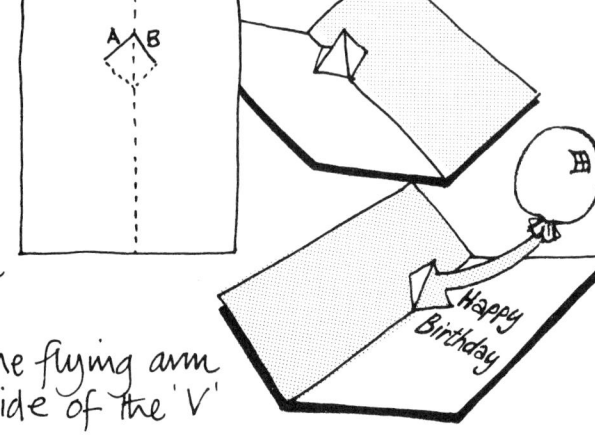

Cut along A and B and fold the 'V' forwards.

Glue the flying arm to one side of the 'V'

Method 2

This method makes use of a separate V-fold which is attached to the backing card about the centre line. The flying arm is then attached as for Method 1.

Cut out and fold the 'V'. Glue it to the backing card.

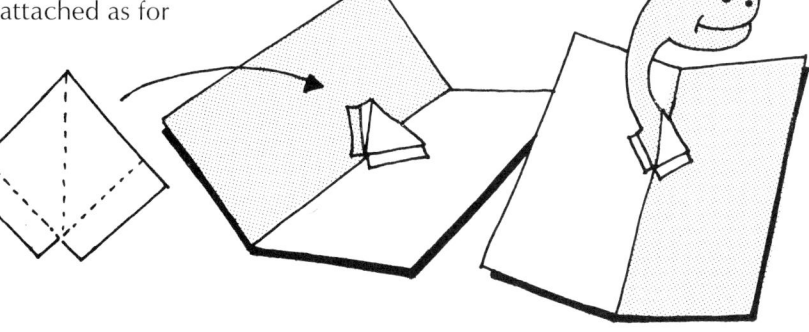

Glue the moving image to the 'V'

Method 3

This method makes use of a V folded into the edge of a horizontal or vertical plane. Again the flying arm is attached to one surface of the V. This method also allows for the image to pop out from behind another layer if desired, which can create an element of surprise.

'V' folds inwards

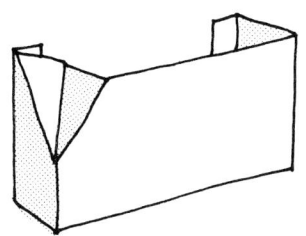

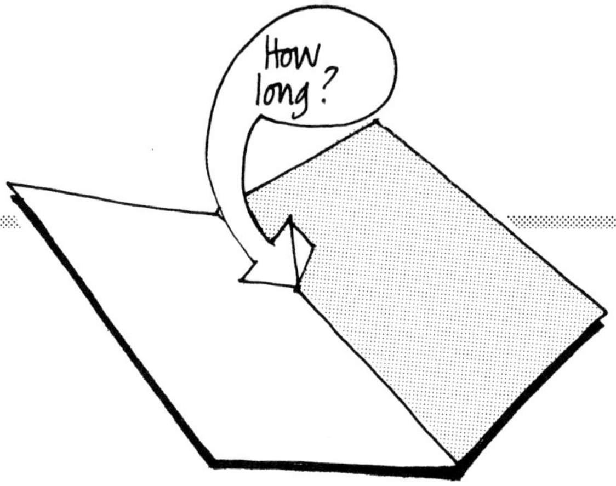

EXPLORATIONS

With a folded A4 sheet as a backing card, make some trial V-folds and flying arms (using any of the previous three methods). Find
■ the position of V-fold which permits the longest flying arm which is still hidden when the card is closed,
■ the shape of V-fold which makes the arm move most, and
■ the biggest and heaviest flying arm which will work.

Experiment with different materials for the flying arm. Try and find materials which can make the arm
■ springy
■ hard to see.

Can you think of ways of using the flying arm movement to activate a switch (a microswitch, for example, or a foil membrane switch)? Could it be opened by using an elastic band?

Look at Method 3. Could you use a flying arm to pull a message from behind a screen?

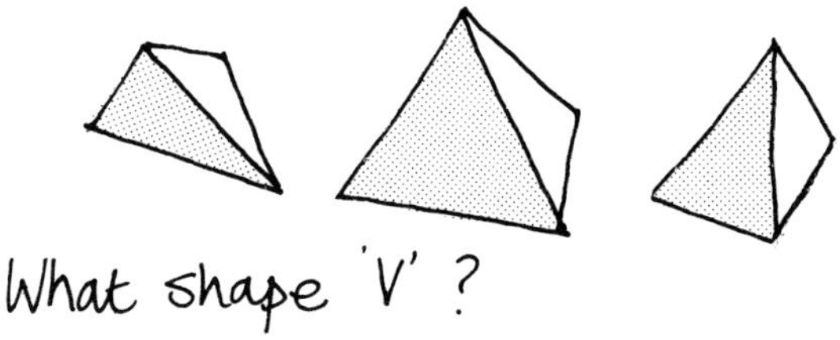

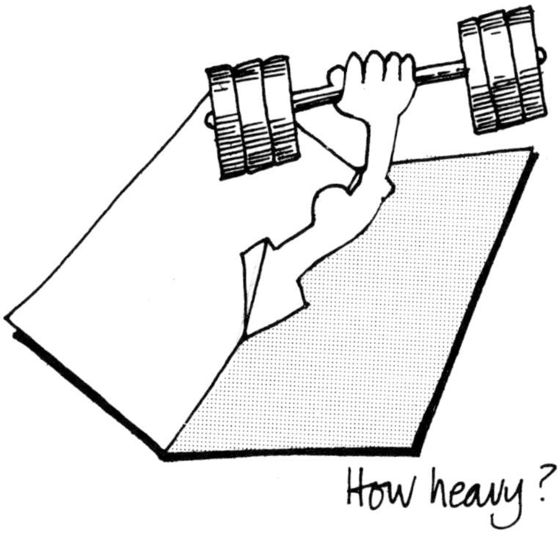

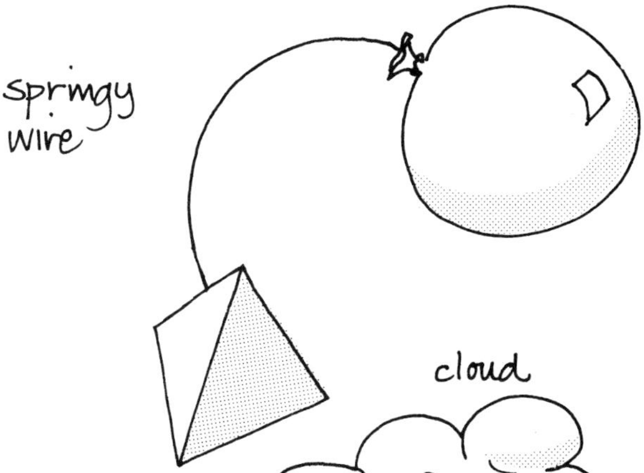

How long?

What shape 'V' ?

How heavy?

springy wire

cloud

clear acetate sheet

Boo!

Card screen glued to parallel surface.

D FORMS

BASIC BOXES

The basic box form is built around a horizontal layer which has sides attached to it, to make a flat-topped square or rectangular box. Only two sides are attached to the base card. The other two sides are folded in line with the centre fold in the base card. When the card or book is closed, these two sides fold, so the whole assembly lies flat.

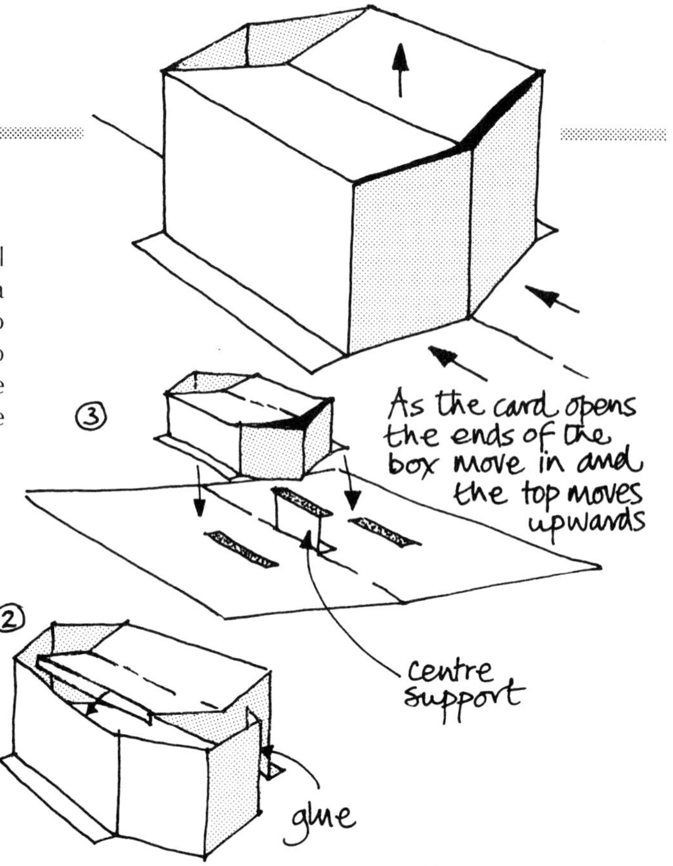

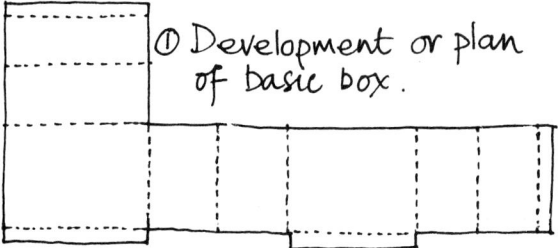

① Development or plan of basic box.

③

②

As the card opens the ends of the box move in and the top moves upwards

centre support

glue

A variation on this approach uses the V-fold principle to form a four-sided open-topped box. Again, only two of the four sides are attached to the backing card with fixing flaps. The other two move freely.

This type of box can be made with a lid by adding two more V-folds inside the box itself. When the sides of the box open out to form the basic square box-shape, these two V-folds are pulled flat to form the top.

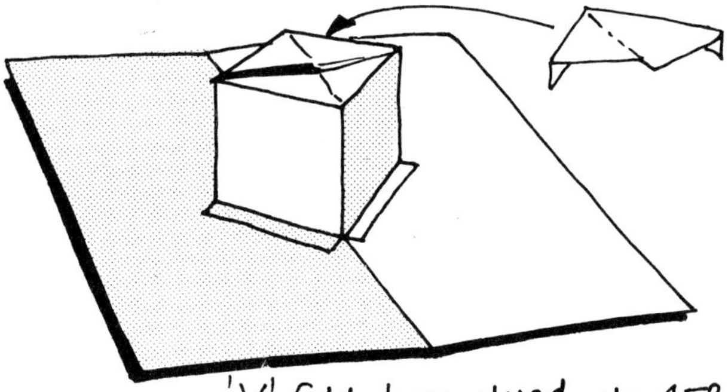

Circular box

You can even make a box which is almost circular. The illustrations show a circle of card to which has been added a continuous strip to form the vertical side. As the card opens the centre support forces the top to open flat, and the edges of the circular top push out the side wall.

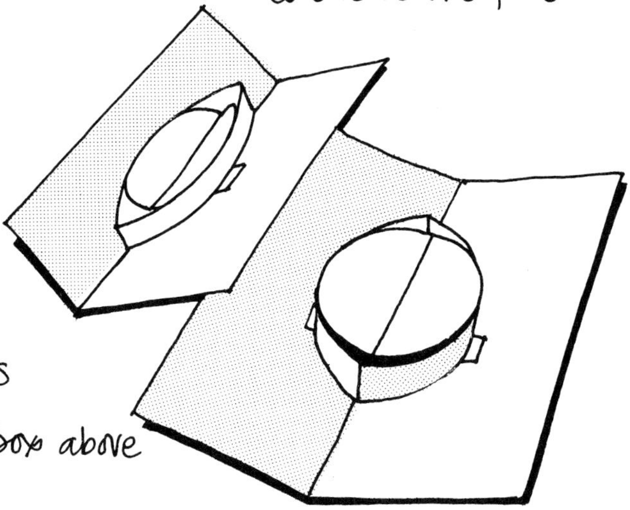

'V' fold box glued at 45° to the centre fold

The circular box works in the same way as the basic rectangular box above

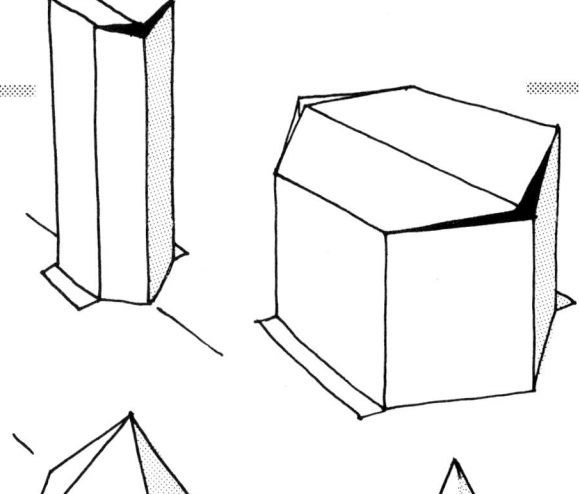

EXPLORATIONS

Can you use the basic box method to make different shapes? Try
■ a tall thin shape,
■ a six-sided shape (hexagon),
■ a pyramid shape, a cone shape.
Does the top have to be flat? Try a tent shape, for example.

Can you make shapes come through the box-top? Try a Jack-in-the-box, in which Jack jumps through the lid when you open the card.

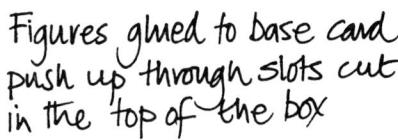

Figures glued to base card push up through slots cut in the top of the box

Tent

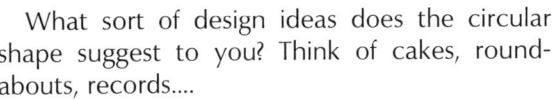

What sort of design ideas does the circular shape suggest to you? Think of cakes, round-abouts, records....

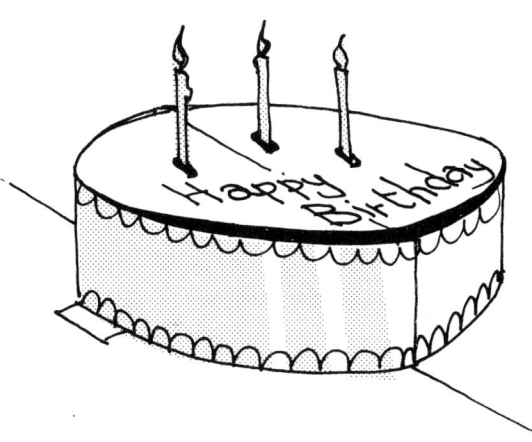

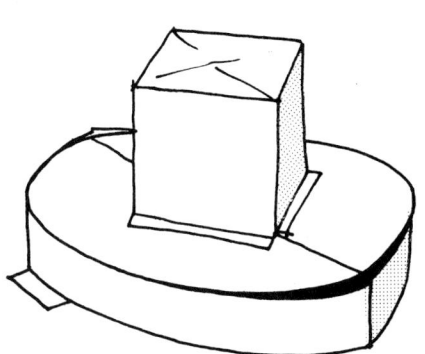

LINEAR MOTION

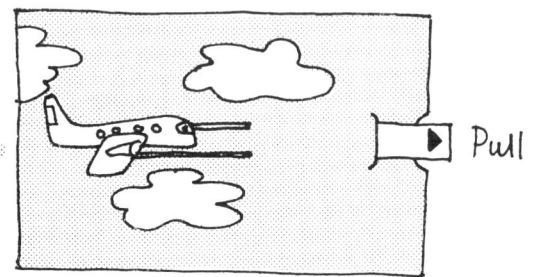

Linear motion is movement which takes place in a straight line. This mechanism is used in a wide range of ways, for different effects, in pop-up books, cards, and other paper engineering examples.

The basic linear motion mechanism makes an image move across a surface, at any angle. To achieve this effect, the user operates a push/pull link. An added element of surprise or interest can be included by making the image come from behind a screen.

In its simplest form, this mechanism involves four main elements—the push/pull link, guides, the backing card (which is part of the mechanism), and the moving image itself.

Because this is a mechanism, in which all the parts have to work together, it must be made accurately. Some parts, like the push/pull link, have to withstand quite large forces, and you must make them stronger and stiffer. You can do this by using thicker card, or by doubling up thin card.

The main problem that you are likely to come across is jamming. To make sure your mechanism doesn't jam, you must

■ make sure all parts fit together accurately, but with enough play to be able to move,
■ make sure that all your guides and slots line up accurately when assembling your mechanism.

And remember, if you're careless with glue, the moving parts of your mechanism won't be able to slide across each other.

The plane moves in a line — the movement is linear

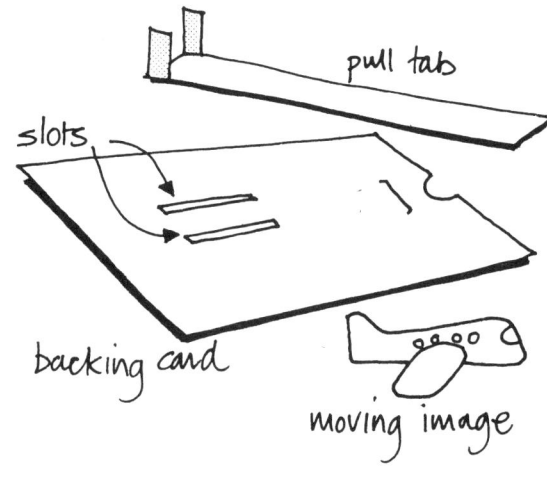

pull tab

slots

backing card

moving image

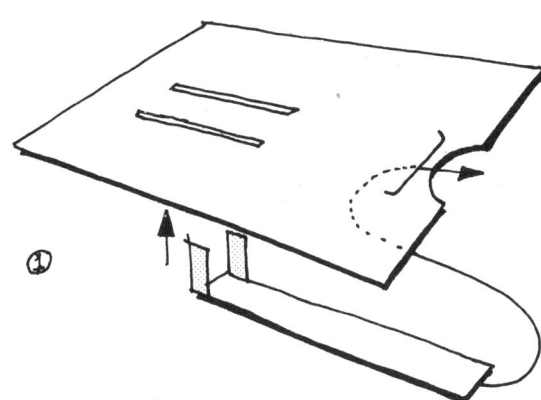

①

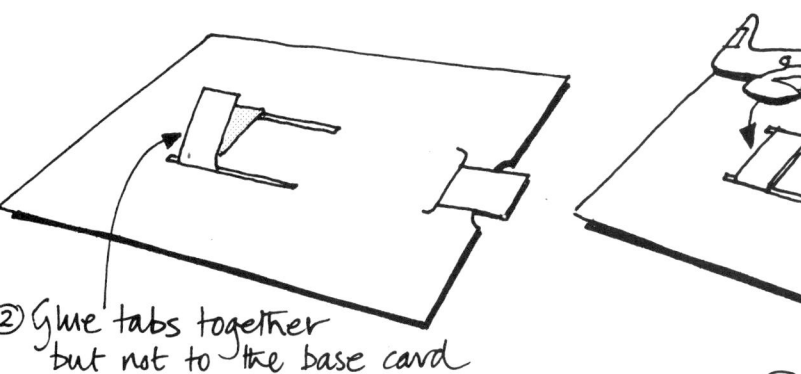

② Glue tabs together but not to the base card
Check that the pull tab moves smoothly

③ Glue moving image to pull tab.

EXPLORATIONS

When you have constructed the basic mechanism (either from a template or by using the information on these pages) think about ways of using it. What kind of images would work well? Can you use more than one screen? Can the screen be pierced or cut—perhaps like a lion's cage, or a gap in the jungle.

Use the mechanism you've made to make a moving image illustrating any one of the themes below.

■ a face which changes expression
■ a chase
■ a surprise greeting

The basic mechanism makes the image move in the direction in which you move the push/pull link. You can reverse the effect using a cord loop as shown below, so that when you pull the link in one direction, the image moves in the other.

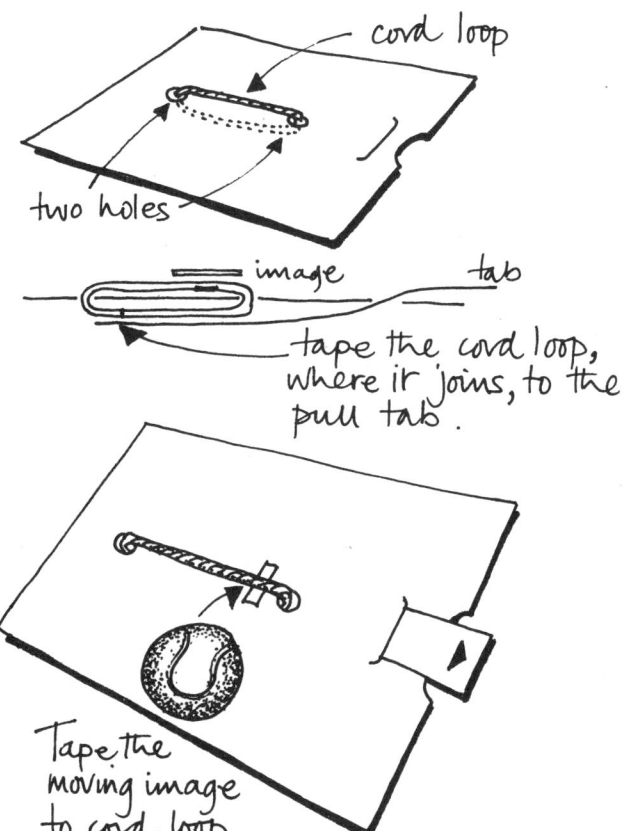

cord loop

two holes

image   tab

tape the cord loop, where it joins, to the pull tab.

Tape the moving image to cord loop

screen   Hello

The face slides out from behind the screen.

How can you change the face? What parts can be made to move?

pull

Does the card have to have a straight edge?

When you've made a working example, think about the following idea. At the moment, it needs a pull to move in one direction and a push to return. Are there ways in which you can use an elastic band to make the mechanism return automatically?

Use this automatic return mechanism to make a moving image which makes people laugh.

Can you think of ways of combining this technique with the others you've seen? Would a horizontal or vertical plane (see pages 6 and 7) support an image which moves?

ROTARY MOTION

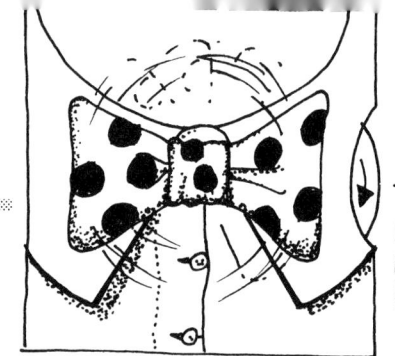

turning here makes the bow tie rotate.

There are two kinds of basic movement in the world of mechanisms—movement in a straight line (linear), and movement in a circular direction around a central pivot. The second is known as **rotary motion**.

Rotary motion has many different applications in paper engineering. Making an image move through an arc (part of a circle) is often preferable to making it move in a straight line. Think about the face which changes expression, or the chase, from the explorations section on page 15—could they be done differently using rotary motion?

From a small circle of card, carefully cut and fold the pivot

Sometimes there is a need to show images or devices which can only move in circles or arcs—like a wheel, the path of the sun or a ball, or the hands of a clock.

To create rotary motion you must know how to make pivot points, and there are several ways of doing this. The most common method—the one you find in pop-up books—uses holes and flaps in the card itself for a smooth-running pivot. Because it's made of card and nothing else, it lies flat, and this makes it important in the design of books and cards.

Push the tabs through the hole in the backing card. DO NOT GLUE THEM TO THE BACKING CARD !!

For a card pivot to work effectively, the central pivot hole needs to be quite large—at least 20 mm. The hole must be a smoothly cut circle, so don't use scissors. Circle cutters can give good results, but they're fiddly to use on holes of this size. The best tool is a wad punch, which is a simple hole-cutter with a circular blade which you hit with a hammer, like a centre punch.

Other pivot methods include paper fasteners, eyelets and click rivets; these can be used to mock up your design ideas even when the final outcome will use a card pivot.

glue moving shape to tabs

glue large disc to the back of the card pivot. The disc should be big enough to allow you to turn it from the edge of the card

paper fastener

eyelet

click or ratchet rivet

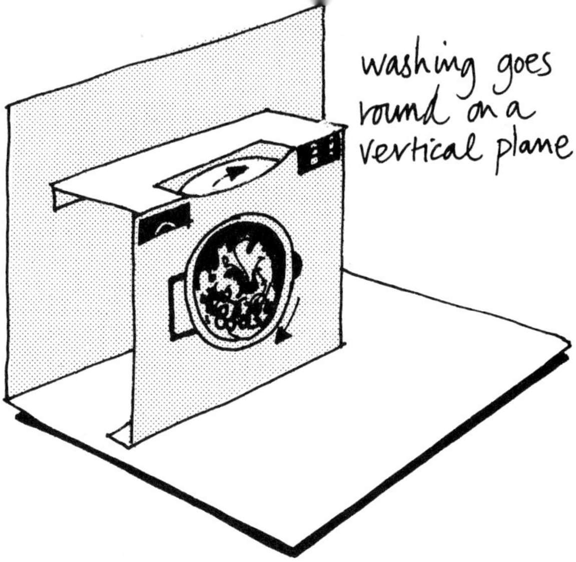

washing goes round on a vertical plane

EXPLORATIONS

The basic card pivot technique is straight-forward to make; put together a simple example now. Once you have made this work, you should be able to develop it in different ways.

Can a pivoted image be mounted on a hori-zontal or vertical plane? What problems can you foresee? Could a rotating image be connected to a sliding image moving in a straight line, as shown on pages 14 and 15? How would you link the two so they move together?

Can a rotating image be made to move into sight from behind a screen? Could it move behind an open window? Can it be made to uncover or hide something as it moves?

Design a moving image based on a fairground theme. Try to bring in at least three of the tech-niques covered so far.

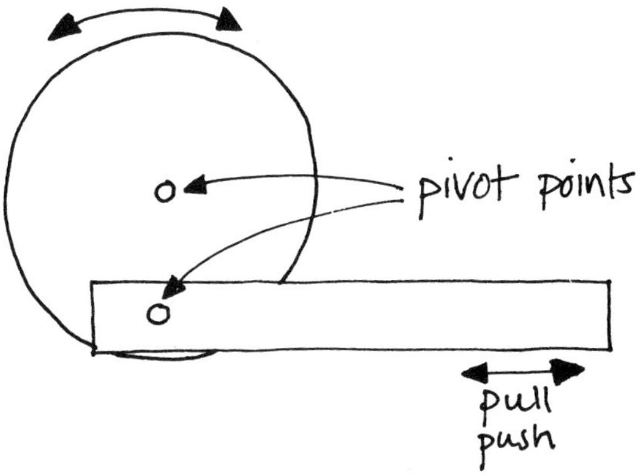

pivot points

pull push

See-saw rotates back and forth

Can you work out how the pickup arm can be made to move to the centre of the record?

45
33

Sony.

17

USING LEVERAGE 1

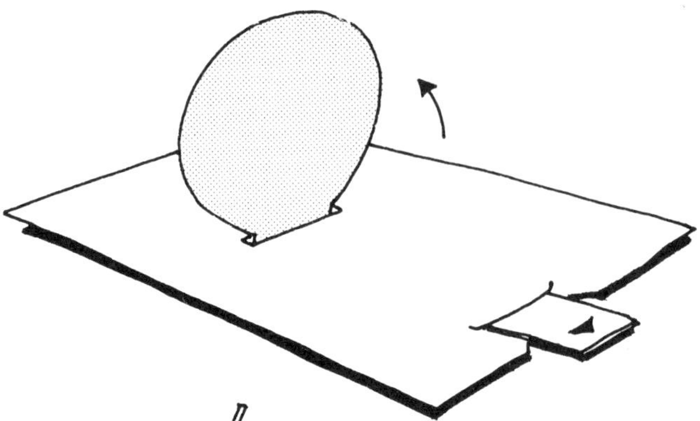

Levers are an important part of many mechanisms. They are used to push or pull with extra force, or to create extra movement. As there is not enough space here for a full explanation of what levers can do, you should ask your teacher about them, or look up 'levers' in a Design and Technology source book.

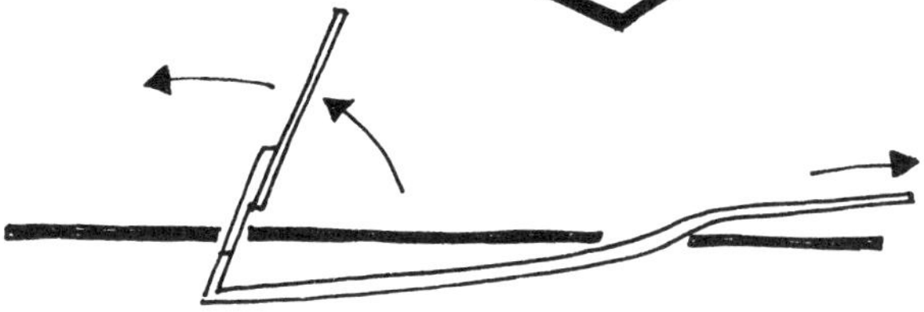

This page shows one important way in which levers can be used in paper or card mechanisms. By this method they can raise a flap or image up from the page; used properly they can hold the image vertical or turn it over like a page in a book.

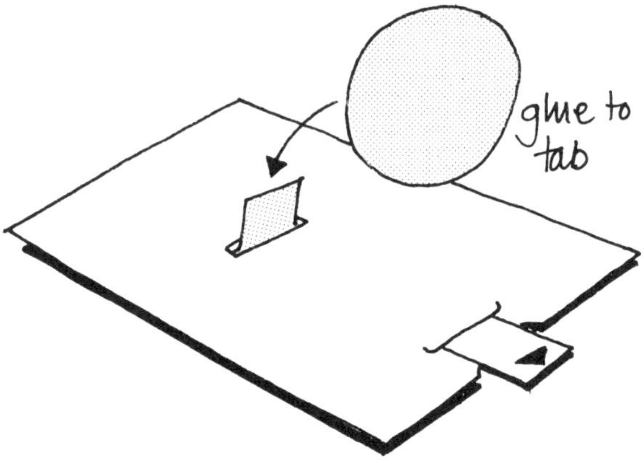

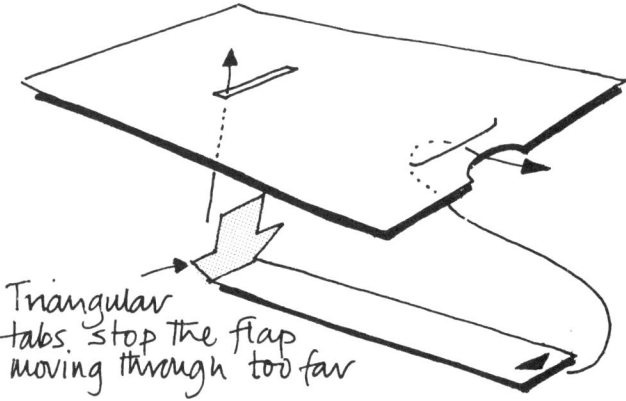

Triangular tabs stop the flap moving through too far

If two flaps are linked so that they move together, then levers can be used to raise a plane above the base surface. Only one of the flaps is used to exert leverage.

The flaps 1 + 2 must be parallel. Flap 1 is glued to the base card.

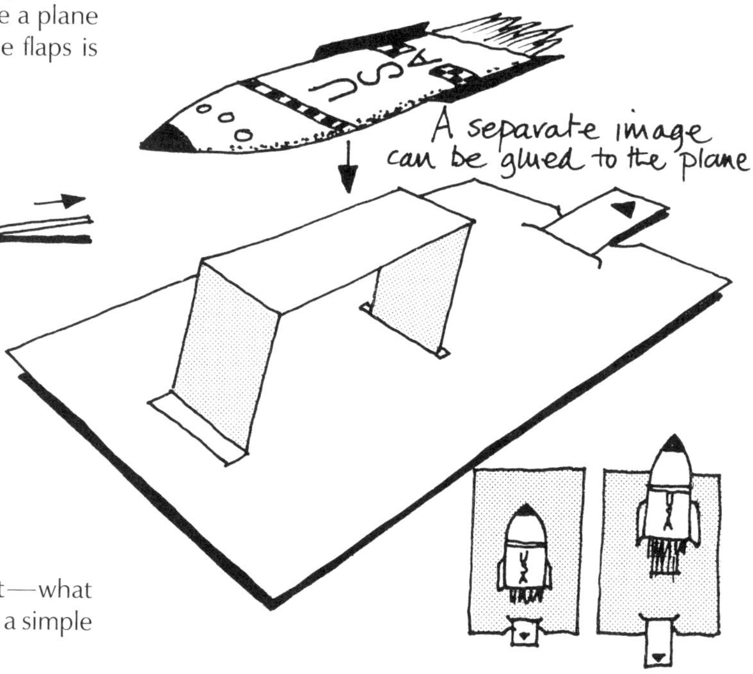

In these examples, the input movement—what you do to make the mechanism work—is a simple push/pull link working in a straight line.

glue to tab

A separate image can be glued to the plane

EXPLORATIONS

Start with a working example of a levered flap and a lifting plane. You may have a template to help you, otherwise draw out a simple one yourself.

What type of lever do both these mechanisms use? What other types of lever are there? (Research this topic in your Design and Technology Resource area).

If the input movement of the push/pull link is linear, in a straight line, what sort of output movement does the moving flap have? Does it move in a straight line, or through an arc? What about the lifting plane?

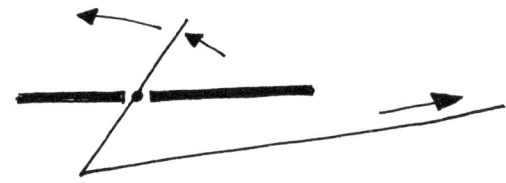

The slot in the backing card acts as the pivot.

It is possible to add more layers to the lifting plane mechanism as you can see from the drawings below.

Is it possible to raise more than one flap? Could one be like a window?

Use one of these two mechanisms to model a design for a page of a young child's pop-up book. The page should help the child connect a picture with a word.

Does the second layer have to be parallel to the top?

Can you use more than two layers or planes?

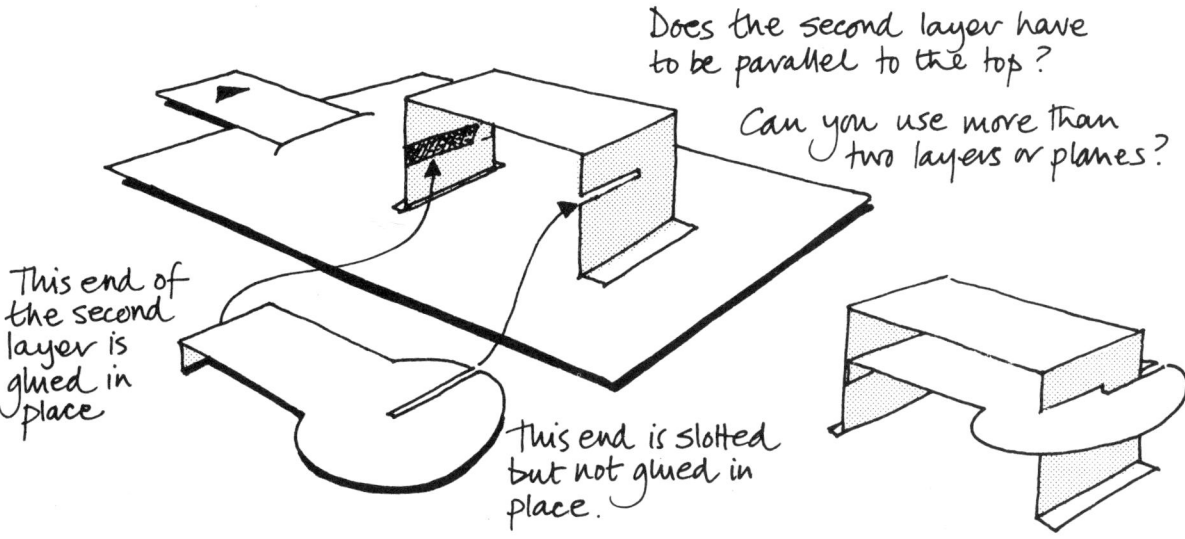

This end of the second layer is glued in place

This end is slotted but not glued in place.

USING LEVERAGE 2

Here is another useful technique which involves levers. In this case the image is not turned over or lifted from the page. Instead it is made to move across the surface of the base card in the path of an arc.

The input movement is again linear, caused by a push/pull link, but the image moves in the opposite direction to the push or pull.

It's important to use the right word to describe the way this mechanism moves. It can move through part of a circle—an arc—but it cannot rotate completely. We cannot call this type of movement rotary, so we use the term **oscillation**, which describes any object which moves backwards and forwards in a regular, predictable way.

Like the previous example, you can connect two or more of the levers together with linkages, so they all move together. It's also possible to connect two levers in such a way that they move in opposite directions at the same time.

As in all lever mechanisms, the position of the pivot point is crucial. Moving it from one place to another can completely reverse the direction of movement, or reduce or increase the distance the mechanism moves.

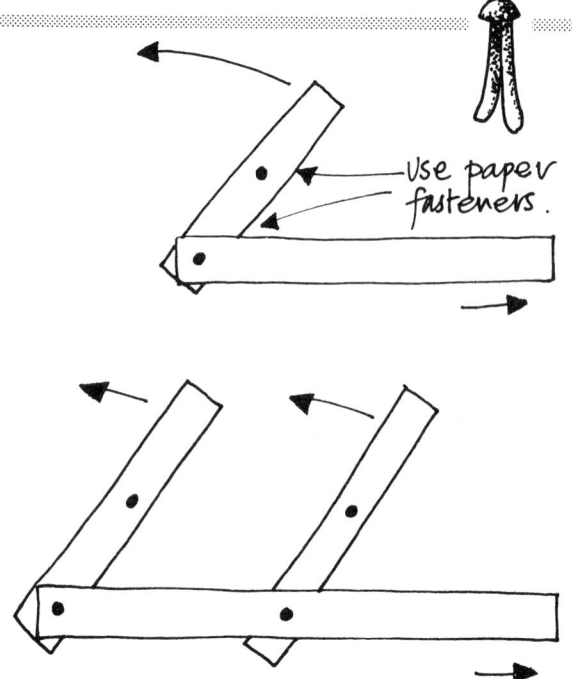

Use paper fasteners.

Normally the lever mechanism is hidden behind the base card, or behind a screen. This often makes it necessary to have a carefully placed slot so that the lever can pass through the base card. The moving image is then attached to the end of the lever.

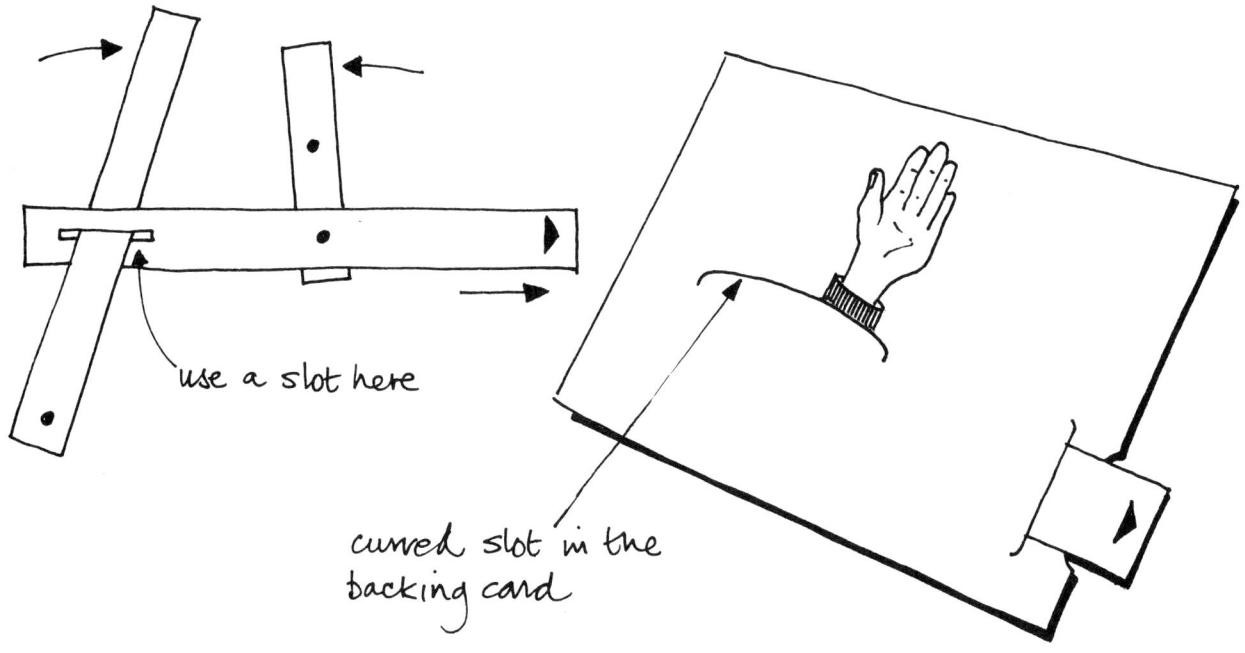

use a slot here

curved slot in the backing card

EXPLORATIONS

Try making a mechanism with two linked levers. When you have made it up you will find that the two levers move together, staying parallel with each other.

How would you make use of this mechanism to create a moving image which suggests
- a frightened animal,
- a storm at sea,
- a pair of hikers?

The mechanism can be modified so that the levers move in opposite directions when the link is pulled. Cut up some spare card into strips and make a rough model of this kind of mechanism. Try using paper fasteners for the pivot points.

What problems do you come across? Are there any parts of the mechanism where these factors are important:
- accuracy,
- play,
- smooth rotation?

Are there any disadvantages in using paper fasteners?

Use this technique to make an amusing image of a dancer, or someone applauding.

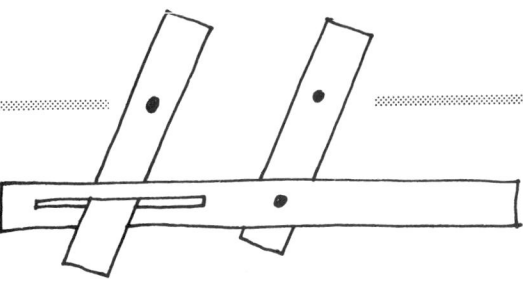

What effect does making the slot longer have?
How could you use this effect?

Can you make both ears move upwards at the same time?

Push/pull tab shows at both ends of the backing card.

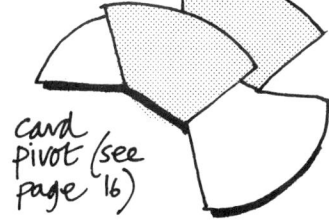

card pivot (see page 16)

Would a card pivot be better for some solutions? Why?

CONTAINERS AND PACKAGES

The most common practical application for paper and card engineering is in the packaging industry.

Straightforward rectangular boxes are not difficult to make—you should be able to find out how they are put together by dismantling a variety of examples.

Here we look at a special technique which you will come across in many real-life examples. The basis of it is the use of curved fold lines to make rigid box shapes which are not simply rectangular. Containers made like this are almost always disposable—they are intended to be thrown away after use—and are stored folded flat until they are used. They are usually assembled by folding along curved score marks, and it is the curved folds which make them rigid.

There are two main problem areas in using this technique. The first is design—how do you decide what shape your box should be, and make your curved folds so that it ends up that shape? You should have a clearer idea of what's involved after you have made up one of the examples shown, but even so, you will probably have to use a trial and error approach at first.

The second problem area arises when you come to scoring the folds. There's no short cut— you can't form the folds without scoring them first, and they have to be scored very accurately. This is where you can make use of a wheeled perforator, but it's often better to use your own purpose-built scoring guide, as shown on page 3.

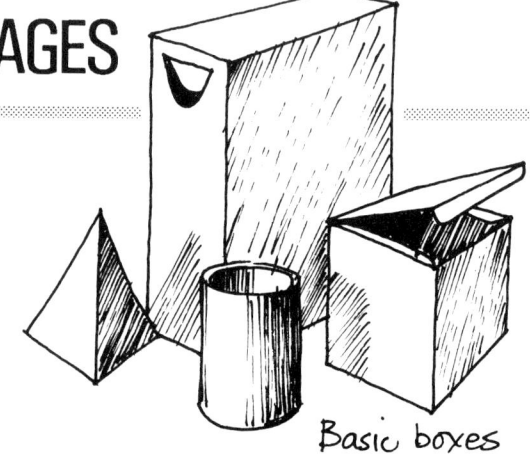

Basic boxes

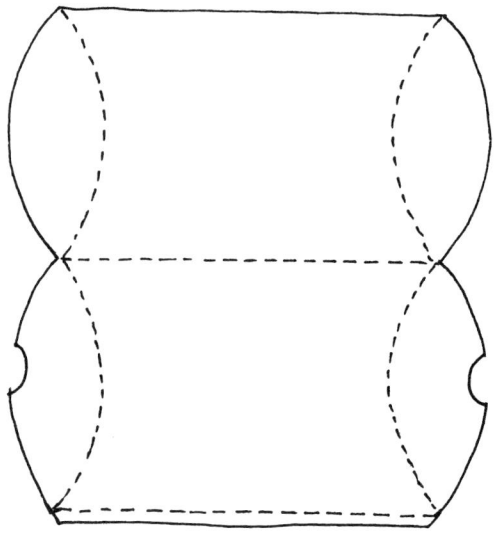

① Cut out and crease along the dotted lines

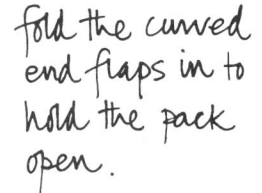

③ fold the curved end flaps in to hold the pack open.

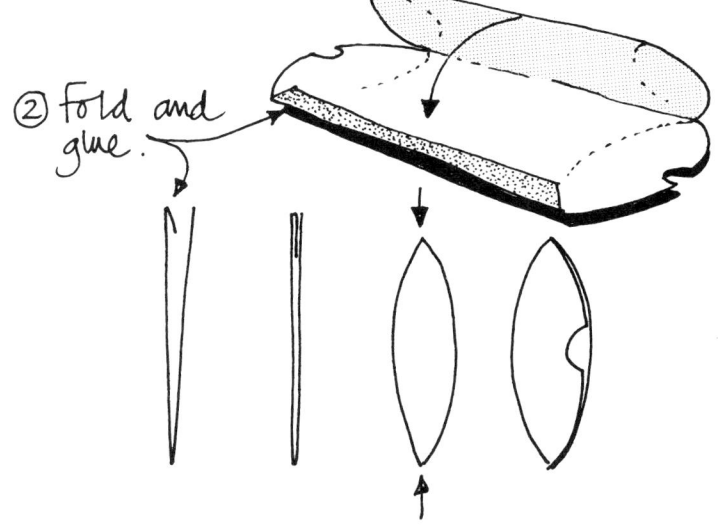

② Fold and glue.

Shown here is a development of a commercially produced card scooper. You may also have a template which helps you make a full-size version.

The word 'development' as it is used here means the whole surface of a hollow container unfolded and laid out flat. This is how all paper or card containers start their existence. The development naturally includes all fixing and joining flaps.

Scale up the illustration in this book, or make one directly from the template. You should appreciate how the curved folds give the structure rigidity, and how they make it snap into position.

Make a collection of all the used card containers you can find which use curved folds. Wherever possible, collect two, so you can dismantle one and keep the other one intact. Notice similarities and differences in the way they are made.

Develop a packaging design which makes use of curved folds to contain one of the following commodities:
- jewellery (a gift box),
- chips,
- a mug or glass,
- pot pourri (find out what it is if you don't know).

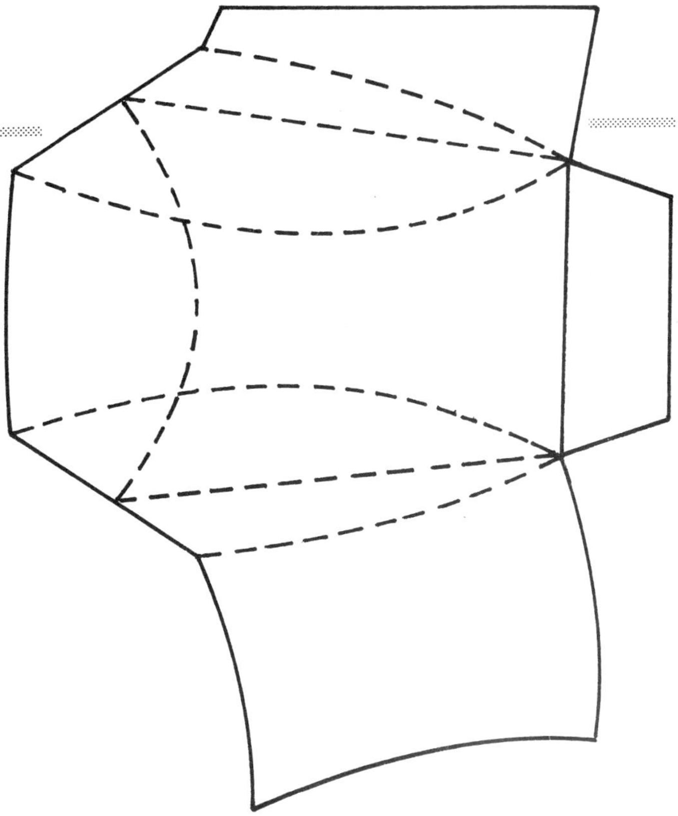

Development of card scooper

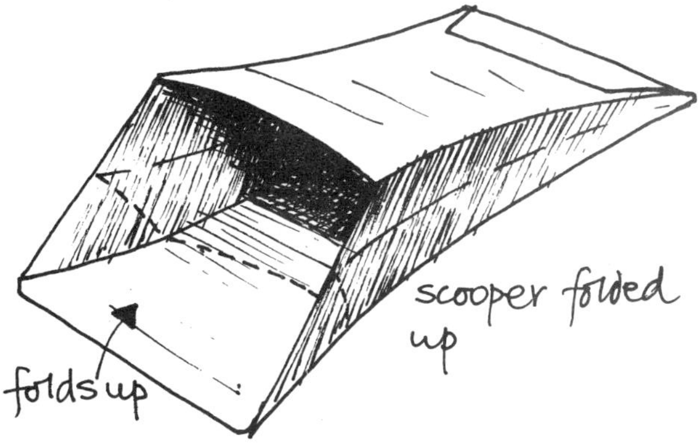

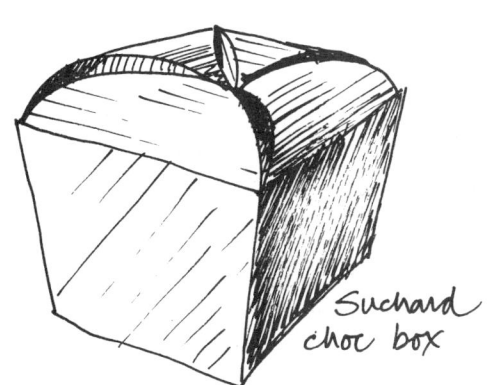

scooper folded up

folds up

McDonald's chip pack.

Suchard choc box

PACKAGING FOOD

This challenge is about packaging food and drink. A moments thought will convince you that this has been a problem area for people throughout our history, and different ages have brought different technologies to bear on the problem.

Paper and card play a major part in modern approaches to this problem. Structures which both protect and help to preserve foodstuffs and drink are made from these materials, and also from thin plastics sheet which behaves in a similar manner. There are also new composite materials like the plastic-coated card used for some drink cartons. Composite materials are materials made from more than one **kind** of substance—e.g. paper and plastic used together.

The food and drink industry uses packaging to such a large extent that it is sometimes criticised for using the earth's resources wastefully. Why do you think this is?

In response, producers and sellers claim that many types of food and drink really do need packaging. Do you think this is justified?

CHALLENGES

Food and drink come from a number of sources. In your area they may be locally grown or processed, or they may be imported from another part of the country or from abroad.

Find out which of these sources is most likely in your locality. Choose one local source of food or drink. This can be a producer (usually a farmer), a processor (e.g. a sweet factory, a creamery, a bakery, a bottling plant), or an importer (e.g. fish or vegetable wholesalers, supermarkets, delicatessens—all of these bring food into an area from elsewhere, so they're all importers).

Identify a food or drink product which would benefit from the right kind of packaging. Summarise

■ your reasons for choosing the product
■ why it needs packaging.

Develop some ideas for packaging your chosen product, bearing in mind

■ quantity per pack,
■ type of protection needed,
■ ease of packing,
■ ease of opening by the customer,
■ cost per pack,
■ information about storage and use.

What else can you think of? Take one of these ideas and develop it into a full-size model of the package, which could be used to show your ideas to the producer, processor or importer of the product.

PACKAGING FRAGILE ITEMS

Think of something fragile, that you've seen in a shop. Now try to imagine its life from the time it came into the world, up to when you saw it. How often do you suppose it has come close to being damaged or broken?

It may well have travelled hundreds or even thousands of miles, been loaded, unloaded, stored in a warehouse. It may have been in a box which was thrown, dropped or stacked underneath other boxes. It may even have survived being picked up by you!

If the object you're thinking of was packaged, you can probably understand why. If it wasn't, then maybe it should have been.

The way fragile items are packaged varies with their value. If each unit has a low value then the packaging will most likely be simple and basic, with little attempt to make it look attractive. Such items will be sold in multiples—think of eggs, or mass-produced glasses.

If each item has a relatively high value then more will be spent on packaging—more time, more effort, better materials. The packaging will be designed more carefully, and will have to do two main jobs.

1) It will have to protect the item from all forces and impacts which normal handling imposes on it.

2) It will help to market the item, to present it in an attractive way and put across ideas about it.

In some cases the packaging has also got a formal function, as a presentation box. A whole range of items, from Easter Eggs to watches, are packaged in this way.

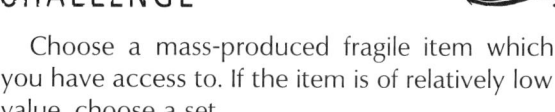

CHALLENGE

Choose a mass-produced fragile item which you have access to. If the item is of relatively low value, choose a set.

Experiment with packaging methods. Use a range of techniques, and make sure that you bear in mind the fact that packaging costs money. Match the techniques and materials you use to the value of what you're packaging.

When you have some structural designs you know will work, think about the following:
How would you market the item you have chosen in a new outlet—a place where it isn't being sold at the moment? Choose a specific place—anything from a railway station buffet to local newsagent. Design a package aimed at this particular environment, which both protects and markets your fragile item.

Easter eggs are very fragile. How can they be protected?

Terry's Moonlight Chocolate box opens like a jacket.

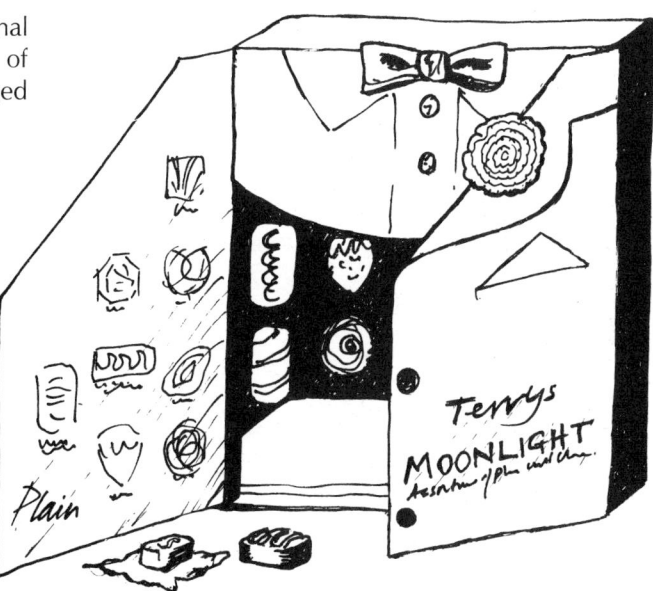

Plain

Terry's MOONLIGHT

UKKI-POPS

Heyyyyyy! You've seen Yukki Pops—course you have. You must have seen the ads. Every 15 minutes on Saturday mornings. You've heard the jingle. 'Yukki-pops, Yukki-pops, really really are the tops'. Course you have. You've heard the catch-phrase. 'Theyyyyyre Yukkeeeee'. **Course** you have.

You **haven't?** Gedoudahere! You must be kidding me. You are, aren't you? OK, OK, I get the message. Let's get on with it.

See, the thing is, they're not selling too well. Can't understand it. Just because we've used a few too many dyes and preservatives—too many E-numbers, is what they're saying. And then again, we use highly refined grain, for that Yukkeee texture, and that means less vitamins and protein. And the sweetener we use being banned in the States didn't help...

Anyway, we need to get the youngsters on our side. Get them begging for Yukki Pops again like the good old days. And that's where you come in. You know you used to be able to get fold-up card models on the back of cereal packets. Boring, weren't they? What we need is something along those lines, but interesting. Clever structures, witty ideas, good graphics—and above all, something which sums up the whole concept of **YUKKI POPS!**

TOURIST GUIDE

Tourism is a major industry—one of the biggest in the UK. Think of the tourist attractions near you. Wherever you live, there are bound to be some.

Tourists very often need information and guidance. What sort of information would tourists need when visiting the attraction shown below?

They might need any of the following
■ a map showing its location,
■ a plan of the site, showing points of interest, main attractions, toilets etc.,
■ souvenirs, brochures, postcards, badges,
■ technical information. Can you think of anything else visitors might want or need?

CHALLENGE

Identify a tourist attraction in your area. Using any of the paper mechanisms or structures you have come across in this book, develop a design for a 3-D pop-up or fold-out tourist guide or brochure which
■ shows the important features of the tourist attraction,

■ gives important information about it visually rather than in words, so that it is useful to foreign tourists, for example.

As you develop your ideas, bear the following in mind:
■ what should the overall size of the guide or brochure be?
■ how can you achieve maximum ease of production?
■ which mechanisms give the effects you want?
■ is it a good idea to use humour?
■ what is the best overall style to use?
■ can you find any examples which help?
■ can you find any effects you would like to imitate?

IN THE WAITING ROOM

It's hard to compare doctors' or dentists' waiting rooms. Most people go to the same doctor or dentist for years, and somehow you get the idea that they all have waiting rooms exactly like the ones you go to.

The jokes don't help—you know, the jokes about out-of-date magazines and so on. In fact, some dentists do a lot to make their waiting rooms more than just a place to bite your nails in. Some doctors do too.

Many of them have play areas for small children. Some of them have a wide selection of up-to-date magazines. And a good many of them have posters and educational displays about health. Often these are advertisements.

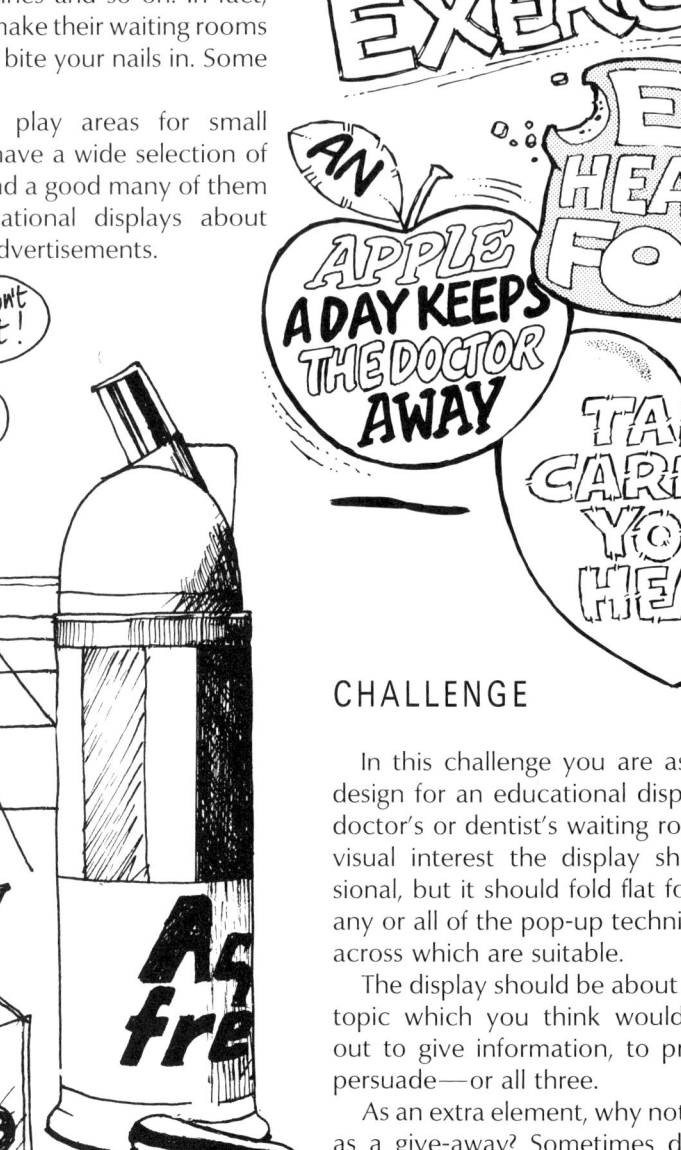

CHALLENGE

In this challenge you are asked to develop a design for an educational display intended for a doctor's or dentist's waiting room. For maximum visual interest the display should be 3-dimensional, but it should fold flat for distribution. Use any or all of the pop-up techniques you've come across which are suitable.

The display should be about any health-related topic which you think would work. It can set out to give information, to provide humour, to persuade—or all three.

As an extra element, why not design the display as a give-away? Sometimes dentists have been known to give presents to children to make their visit more pleasant. Perhaps your display could have a miniature version—simplified, maybe—to meet this purpose.

ERSUASION

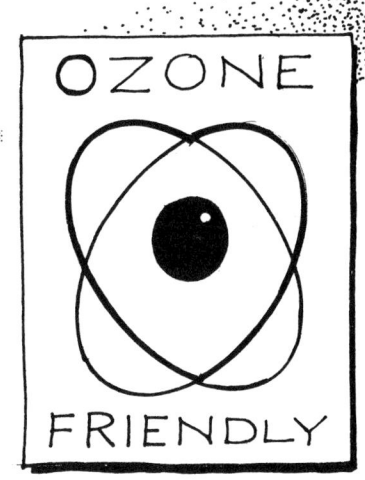

You may have noticed that a major use of card and paper is to persuade. Every day, many people receive junk mail. Everywhere you look, advertisements look back at you. Every time you go into a shop, you're surrounded by hundreds of items, every one of which is packaged in a way that says 'buy me, buy me'.

Paper engineering is often used alongside other means for achieving this. Clever packages and attractive displays play their part.

Not all advertising is about selling, though. Sometimes advertisements are placed to communicate other things. Public service advertisements communicate information. You may have seen the kind of advertisement that looks like a petition, in which a number of people who all believe the same thing let their names appear in print, as a way of putting across their point of view.

Charities, and organisations whose aim is to change the law, or people's behaviour, also advertise. Oxfam, for example, advertises for support. ASH, or Action on Smoking and Health, advertises its point of view. These advertisements are often to do with **campaigns**, in which organisations or groups try to change society, for what they feel is the public good.

CHALLENGE

Is there a campaign about which you feel strongly? Is there some change you would like to see made, even if no campaign exists for it at the moment?

Design a pop-up display (or perhaps a pop-up card mailshot) which sets out to persuade, to put across a point of view. Try to get the most powerful effects you can.

URPRISE!

CHALLENGE 1

Design a surprise greeting card for a friend (or foe). Make the action of the card (the movement of the image) say something about your relationship with whoever it's for. Use the card to **tell** them something.

CHALLENGE 2

Create a pop-up image which gives you a delayed surprise rather than an immediate one. Use one of the lever-operated movements you have come across in this book, or a technique you have discovered elsewhere.

CHALLENGE 3

Use the theme of 'surprise' in a pop-up invitation card. Try a face in which the mouth drops open, or someone being knocked over with a feather—the possibilities are endless.

Little Miss Muffet
Sat on a tuffet...

Down came a
SPIDER!

CHALLENGE 4

How many stories can you think of in which a character gets a surprise. There are thousands. How about Goliath, when the stone hit his forehead? Or the dragon, when St. George...?

Make a pop-up illustration for any well-known fictional situation you can think of in which a character gets a (possibly nasty) surprise.

MENU

Eating out in the UK is changing rapidly. There's more choice than there used to be, and generally, a better standard of service. The biggest change is in the development of chains of different types of eating places which offer the same food, of the same quality, in the same way, in every branch.

This type of eating house is very popular. Why do you think this is?

One very noticeable aspect of cafés or restaurants like this is the way they look and feel very similar, wherever they are. A Little Chef in Scotland is just like a Little Chef in Kent. McDonald's and Pizzaland hardly vary at all; you must be able to think of other examples.

How is this achieved? The décor, furniture and fittings are obviously important elements of the interior design of such places. Just as important, though less obvious, are the details. And one of the most important of the details—the key one, from the customer's point of view—is the menu.

Pizza

CHALLENGE 1

Either on your own, or with a group of friends, develop an idea for a chain of imaginary eating houses. There is no need to be too serious.

Now, on your own, develop an idea for a pop-up menu for such an establishment. The key purpose of the menu will be to show off the new children's menu, designed to bring in more family custom.

CHALLENGE 2

A young couple have invested all their savings in converting an old water-mill into a riverside restaurant. They have asked you to design a pop-up feature menu.

They offer a very small range of very high-class French dishes and sweets, all with a river connection (trout, duck and so on). Every main dish should have its own pop-up feature.

Make sure you spell the names of the meals properly, and find out what the dishes are actually like before you start.

Three fold menu using flaps.

LOCKS

Quartz clock movements are easy to get hold of these days, and they're relatively cheap.

Many of the structures you've already made from paper or card let you build structures of great strength and rigidity. It would not be difficult, for example, to build a simple rigid box-shape and mount a clock-movement inside it.

But this challenge is not simply about designing and making a clock base from card. That's part of it, of course, but there's more.

One of the more interesting features of paper engineering is the way it goes beyond simple boxes and packets, to use paper and card in clever, new, exciting ways.

Sometimes—in the more complex pop-up books, for example—the forms are as much *sculpted* as engineered.

And that's the added dimension of this challenge. You'll need a clock movement, of course. And patience, because you'll try ideas that don't work. Your aim is to make a clock by engineering, or sculpting, or both, that is truly practical, and at the same time exciting, innovative and interesting.

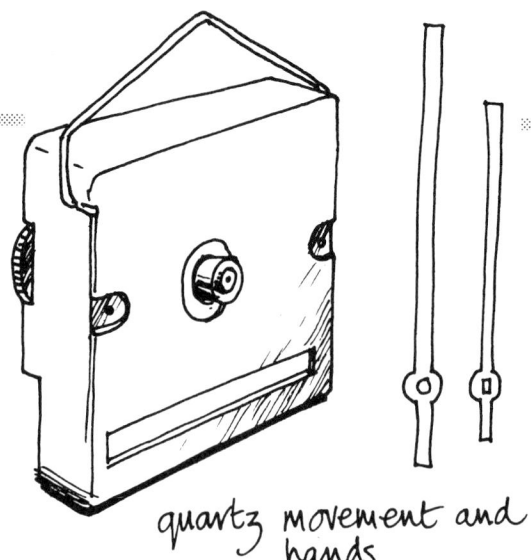

quartz movement and hands

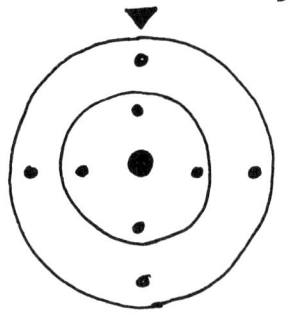 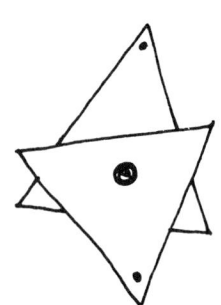

Do the hands have to be strips of metal? Could they be discs of card? Could they be triangular?

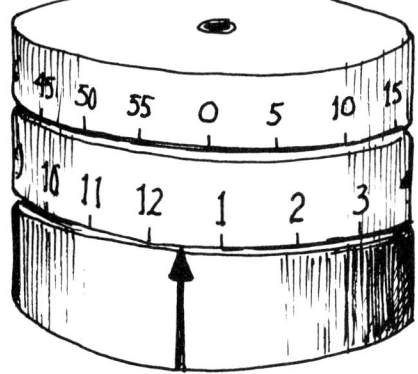

The mechanism could be used horizontally instead of vertically

Where is the clock to be used?
Who is it for?
Does it have to give a precise time or approximate time?

These considerations will affect your design.

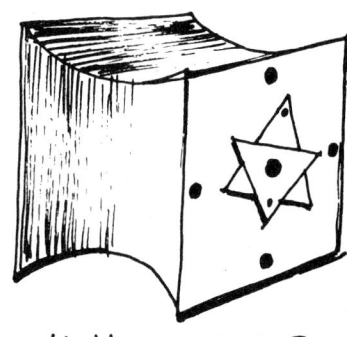

How can you divide a clock face?
How many ways can you think of?

Cover photograph by *Ellen Schuster*, The Image Bank. **Cartoons** by *Pavely Arts*
Illustrations by *Peter Gowers*.